New Worlds

Nick Hunter

www.raintreepublishers.co.uk
Visit our website to find out more information about Raintree books.

To order:
☎ Phone 0845 6044371
🖷 Fax +44 (0) 1865 312263
🖳 Email myorders@raintreepublishers.co.uk

Customers from outside the UK please telephone +44 1865 312262

Raintree is an imprint of Capstone Global Library Limited, a company incorporated in England and Wales having its registered office at 7 Pilgrim Street, London, EC4V 6LB – Registered company number: 6695582

Text © Capstone Global Library Limited 2013
First published in hardback in 2013
Paperback edition first published in 2014

Edited by Rebecca Rissman, Dan Nunn, and Catherine Veitch
Designed by Cynthia Della-Rovere
Levelling by Jeanne Clidas
Picture research by Elizabeth Alexander
Production by Victoria Fitzgerald
Originated by Capstone Global Library
Printed and bound in China by CTPS

ISBN 978 1 406 24189 1 (hardback)
16 15 14 13 12
10 9 8 7 6 5 4 3 2 1

ISBN 978 1 406 24196 9 (paperback)
17 16 15 14 13
10 9 8 7 6 5 4 3 2 1

British Library Cataloguing in Publication Data
Hunter, Nick.
New worlds. -- (Explorer tales)
910.9-dc22
A full catalogue record for this book is available from the British Library.

Acknowledgements
We would like to thank the following for permission to reproduce photographs: Alamy pp. 11 (© Kadokawa/Ancient Art & Architecture Collection), 13 (© 19th era 2), 15 (© Classic Image); Corbis pp. 6 (© Nick Rains), 8, 19 (© Heritage Images), 24 (© Bettmann), 27 (© Jeffrey Rotman); Getty Images pp. 5 (Nordic Photos), 7 (The Bridgeman Art Library), 9 (Science & Society Picture Library), 10 (Stock Montage), 12 (DEA Picture Library), 16 (Stock Montage), 17 (SuperStock), 20 (Hulton Archive), 22 (Archive Photos), 25 (Keystone-France/Gamma-Keystone); Photolibrary p. 23 (LENARTOWSKI); Shutterstock pp. 4 (© sdecoret), 21 (© Ekaterina Pokrovsky); Superstock p. 14 (© age footstock).

Cover photographs of Captain James Cook reproduced with permission of Alamy (© Lebrecht Music and Arts Photo Library); a double hemisphere world map, 1746, reproduced with permission of Sanders of Oxford, rare prints & maps (www.sandersofoxford.com); Australia as seen from space reproduced with permission of Shutterstock (© Joao Virissimo). Background photograph of East Asia from space reproduced with permission of Shutterstock (© Anton Balazh).

Contents

Some words are shown in bold, **like this**. You can find out what they mean by looking in the glossary.

Finding new worlds

Many **ancient** peoples thought that planet Earth was flat. The ancient Greeks were the first people to say that Earth was round like a ball.

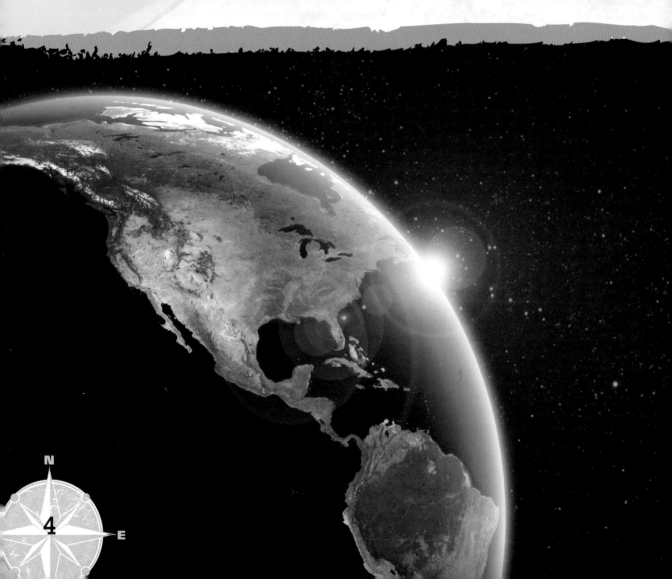

DID YOU KNOW?

The **Vikings** believed the world was flat, but Leif Eriksson was not afraid. Leif kept sailing until he became the first European to land in North America, in around AD 1000.

Viking longship

5

The spice of life

European explorers searched for new ways to reach the **Spice Islands** of the East.

Hundreds of years ago, explorers did not just travel to see new places. They went to find spices or gold that would make them rich.

DID YOU KNOW?

Europeans needed spices for their food. They had no fridges and meat had to be stored through the winter. Spices would make the rotting meat taste a little better.

Sailing into danger

Explorers who set out to discover new worlds faced many dangers. There were no maps to follow. They did not know who or what they might meet. Many explorers never made it back home again.

DID YOU KNOW?

Early explorers believed that anyone who sailed south of the **equator** would be boiled alive because of the heat.

9

Marco and the Mongols

The fearsome **Mongol** warriors built a huge **empire** across Asia in the 1200s. Marco Polo was an explorer. He was about 17 when he left Venice, in Italy. He headed for the centre of Mongol power in China.

Marco Polo

Marco Polo told stories of Emperor Kublai Khan's great feasts, when 6,000 people could fit into the Khan's banquet hall.

11

New discoveries

When Polo returned to Venice, he had many amazing stories to tell. He spoke of money made of paper and stones that burned better than wood. We now know these stones were coal.

Venice

DID YOU KNOW?

Some explorers made up tales about their travels. *The Travels of Sir John Mandeville* told stories of people with heads in their chests!

A very curious man

Ibn Battutah left his home in Morocco, Africa, in 1325. He travelled more than 120,700 kilometres around the **Islamic** world from Africa to China. He had lots of luck on his travels, surviving shipwrecks, **plague**, and violent rulers.

Battutah travelled across hot deserts.

DID YOU KNOW?
During cold winters, Ibn Battutah wore so many clothes that he could not even get on his horse!

The long way round

Christopher Columbus knew how he was going to make his fortune. In 1492, he set sail from Spain to find a new sea route to China.

Christopher Columbus

Columbus thought China was about 5,633 kilometres from Spain. After weeks at sea, he began to have doubts. There was ocean as far as the eye could see, and the crew was restless. Finally, they saw land.

What Columbus found

Columbus was thousands of kilometres from China! He had landed in the Bahamas. As he searched the islands for gold, one ship was wrecked. Then there was a huge storm on his journey home. Columbus was lucky to survive.

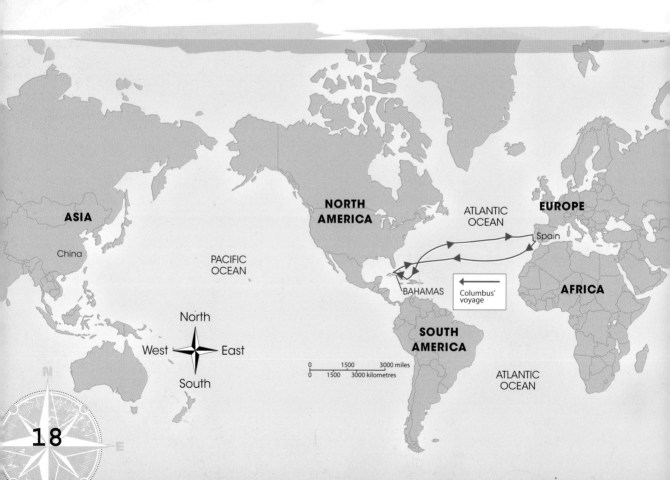

ASIA

China

PACIFIC OCEAN

NORTH AMERICA

ATLANTIC OCEAN

EUROPE

Spain

BAHAMAS

Columbus' voyage

AFRICA

North

West — East

South

SOUTH AMERICA

0   1500   3000 miles
0   1500   3000 kilometres

ATLANTIC OCEAN

Many local people who welcomed Columbus were killed by the new diseases the Europeans brought with them.

Ferdinand's full circle

In 1519, Ferdinand Magellan's journey from Spain to find the **Spice Islands** was in trouble from the start. One of the captains was **executed** when he tried to turn back.

Magellan's ships became the first European ships to cross the Pacific Ocean.

DID YOU KNOW?

Magellan's crew saw new creatures such as penguins and fur seals.

Pacific problems

Magellan's crew was hit by war, disease, and **mutinies**. In 1522, just one ship returned to Spain loaded with spices. Only 17 out of 277 sailors completed the first voyage around the world.

Magellan was killed in a battle on the Philippine Islands.

DID YOU KNOW?

Magellan's starving crew ate leather and biscuit crumbs crawling with worms. If they were lucky, they caught a rat.

Welcome to Hawaii!

Captain James Cook mapped Tahiti, Australia, and many other new lands in the Pacific Ocean during three long voyages. In 1779, Cook was killed by islanders in Hawaii.

Captain James Cook

This picture shows Cook's ship in the icy Pacific Ocean.

What's left to explore?

The surface of our planet has been mapped by explorers. There are still things to explore, though. Humans have not yet fully explored Earth's deepest oceans or the thickest areas of rainforest.

DID YOU KNOW?

Some people believe there are creatures we have not yet discovered. Could you be the explorer who finds the truth?

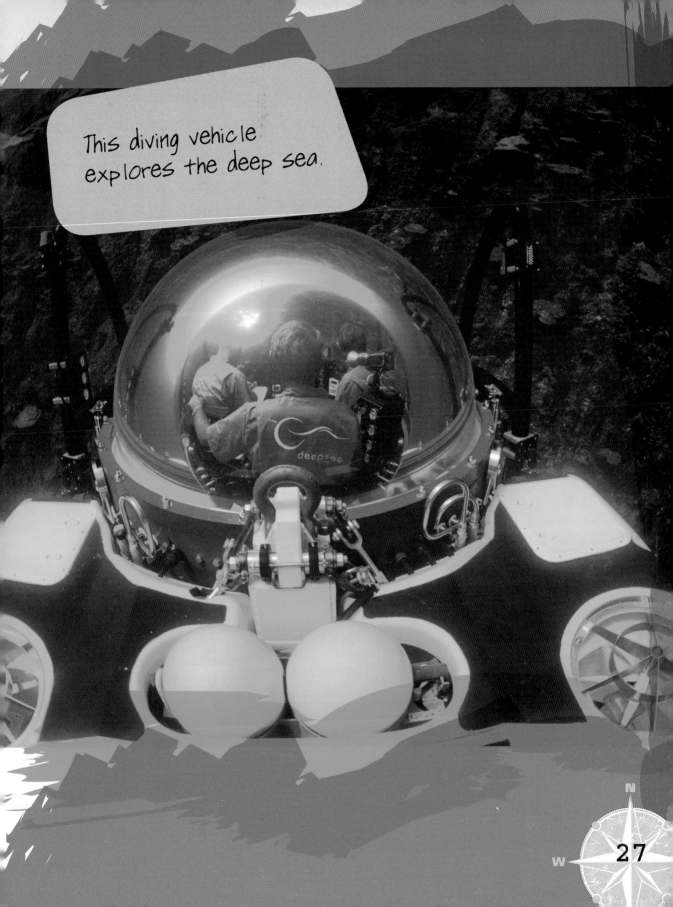

This diving vehicle explores the deep sea.

Timeline

AD 1000 Leif Eriksson's **expedition** to North America takes place.

1271 Marco Polo (lived about 1254–1324) sets out on his journey to China.

1325 Ibn Battutah (1304–about 1369) begins to explore the **Islamic** world.

1492 Christopher Columbus (1451–1506) discovers the islands of the Caribbean while looking for a route to China.

1522 Ferdinand Magellan (1480–1521) becomes the first person to sail around the world.

1776 James Cook's (1728–1779) third voyage to explore the northern Pacific Ocean takes place. Cook is killed by islanders in Hawaii in 1779.

Becoming an explorer

Many scientists are really explorers. They explore the world of animals, plants, or the oceans and find new things all the time.

To become an explorer, you will need to:

- study hard and become an expert
- be curious about the world
- have training to survive in dangerous places, from the frozen polar regions to the top of a bubbling volcano.

Glossary

ancient lived or existed a long time ago

empire countries or lands ruled by another country

equator imaginary line around the middle of Earth, separating north and south

execute kill

expedition journey for a particular reason, such as to discover new lands

Islamic following the religion of Islam

Mongols people who ruled a huge empire in Asia and eastern Europe from around 1200 to the mid-1300s

mutiny rebellion, especially by soldiers or sailors against their officers

plague serious disease that spreads rapidly and kills many people

Spice Islands large group of islands in Asia, now known as the East Indies. The islands were famous as the source of many spices. Spices are dried parts of plants that are used to flavour food.

Vikings people who lived in northern Europe between about 750 and 1050. Viking warriors explored and raided many parts of Europe.

Find out more

Books

Adventures of Marco Polo (Graphic History), Roger Smalley (Raintree, 2012)

Great Explorers, Jim Pipe (Oxford University Press, 2008)

Intrepid Explorers (Horrible Geography), Anita Ganeri and Mike Phillips (Scholastic, 2010)

Websites

www.enchantedlearning.com/explorers

You can find biographies and pictures of many different explorers on this website.

www.nmm.ac.uk/TudorExploration/ NMMFLASH/index.htm

Visit this website to discover more about Tudor explorers.

Index